HISTORY IN FOCUS 1

Pre-history to Roman Britain

Ray Mitchell and
Geoffrey Middleton

Illustrated by
Michael Whittlesea and
Illustra Design Limited

Longman

Introduction

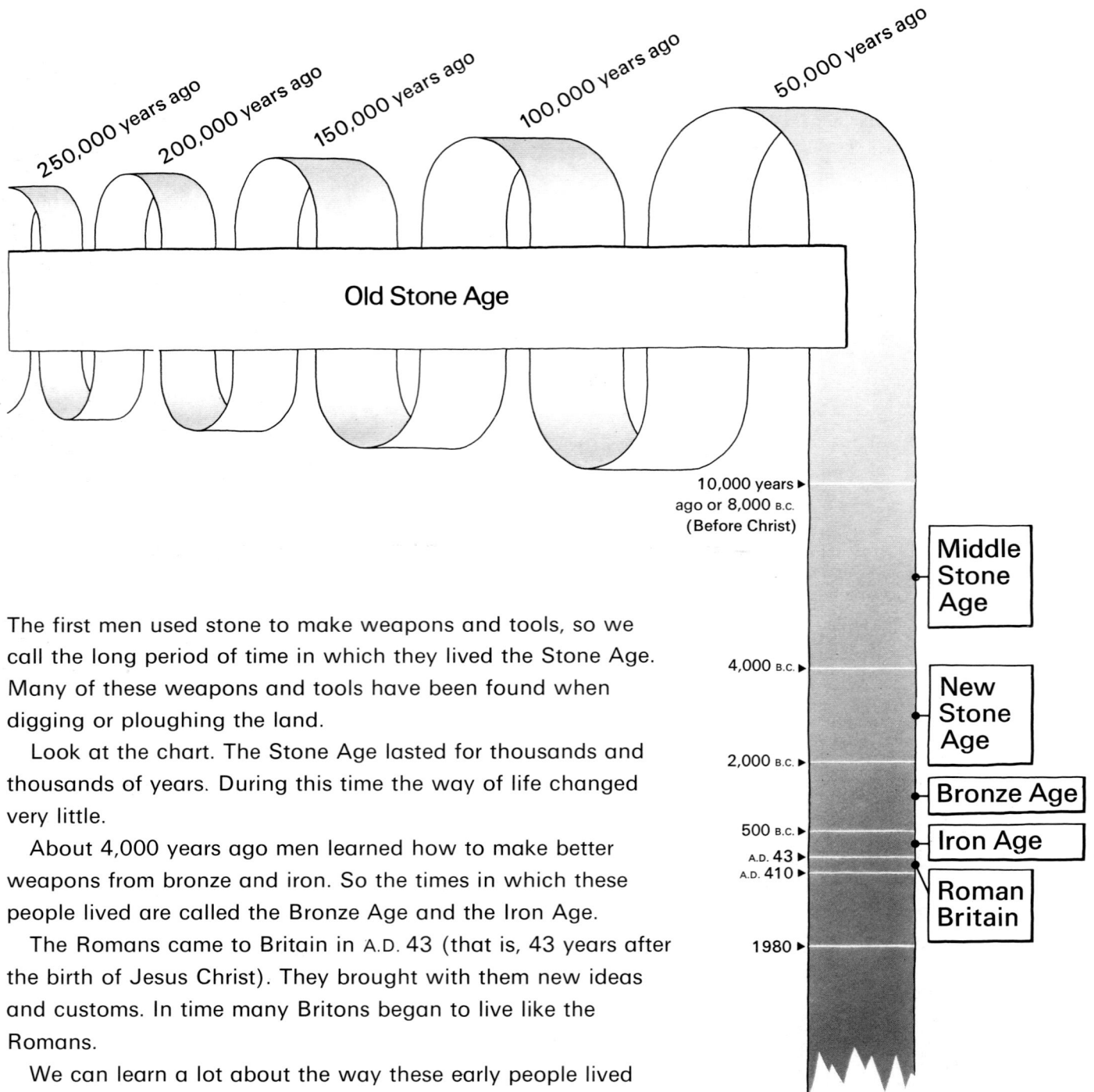

250,000 years ago   200,000 years ago   150,000 years ago   100,000 years ago   50,000 years ago

Old Stone Age

10,000 years ▶
ago or 8,000 B.C.
(Before Christ)

4,000 B.C. ▶

2,000 B.C. ▶

500 B.C. ▶
A.D. 43 ▶
A.D. 410 ▶

1980 ▶

Middle Stone Age

New Stone Age

Bronze Age

Iron Age

Roman Britain

The first men used stone to make weapons and tools, so we call the long period of time in which they lived the Stone Age. Many of these weapons and tools have been found when digging or ploughing the land.

Look at the chart. The Stone Age lasted for thousands and thousands of years. During this time the way of life changed very little.

About 4,000 years ago men learned how to make better weapons from bronze and iron. So the times in which these people lived are called the Bronze Age and the Iron Age.

The Romans came to Britain in A.D. 43 (that is, 43 years after the birth of Jesus Christ). They brought with them new ideas and customs. In time many Britons began to live like the Romans.

We can learn a lot about the way these early people lived from the things they used. Weapons, tools and pictures have been found and put in museums for us to look at. There are photographs of many of these very old things in this book. Pictures have been drawn to show how we think these things were used and how the people might have lived.

The Old Stone Age
Early man

People have not always lived, worked and dressed like we do today. And they have not always looked like us.

Here is a picture of some people who lived in the entrances to caves in China about 500,000 years ago.

Rhinoceros

Elephant

Find the man dragging a dead deer to the cave. These people were hunters. They had to hunt and kill wild animals for food — deer, horses, pigs, buffaloes, even elephants and rhinoceroses. Hunting was dangerous, for the men had only wooden spears made from branches of trees.

They also ate nuts and berries. Sometimes, too, they killed other men and ate their brains.

Look at the man in the centre of the picture. He is hitting one stone on another to make a rough stone tool. He needed these stone tools to cut up the dead animals, to strip off their skin and fur and to tear the meat from the bones.

The woman is putting wood on the fire. These people had discovered how to make fire. Fire kept them warm, cooked their food and frightened away wild animals.

For thousands of years men had to make their weapons and tools from wood, bones and stones. This part of the story or history of men is called the Old Stone Age.

Above is a deer-hunt by the River Thames at Swanscombe in Kent, about 250,000 years ago. Britain was joined by land to Europe. We believe these were some of the first men to live in Britain.

Even by this time, the way of life had not changed very much. These early people still hunted animals and collected wild berries.

Look for:

—the hunters

—their wooden spears. (They also may have used slings.)

—the deer.

The hunters waited in the trees until the animals came to the river to drink. Then they rushed out to kill them.

Find also:

—the elephant tusk half-buried in the sand. In those days there
 were elephants in Britain by the River Thames.

—the skull of a wild bull

—the stones lying on the sand. These were hand-axes thrown
 away by other hunters.

These hunters had to wander from place to place, hunting and searching for food. They may have built shelters with branches of trees.

One of the hand-axes found at Swanscombe. The hand-axe was the main tool of the early hunters. It was used to kill animals, clean skins, cut meat, dig up roots and shape wood.

This family lived in Gibraltar, about 50,000 years ago. There is snow on the Spanish hills and the man is pulling an animal skin around his shoulders to keep warm.

The woman is scraping a deer skin with a flint scraper. She also used sharpened stones to pierce and cut animals and to dig out roots. These people are called Neanderthal Men.

Look for:
—the wooden spear and the things caught that day
—the caves where they lived in cold weather and the fire. In fine weather they lived outside.

Now look at the picture below of a family group of people in France, about 12,000 years ago. The hunters have returned from a hunt. On the ground is an antelope's skull and over their shoulders the hunters carry chamois and arctic foxes.

Find the fish which have been speared in the river and the reindeer antlers on the floor.

These people were still hunters and food gatherers, but they look more like us. The men have learned how to make better tools of stone, bone and antler. The women made clothes of fur and leather and knew how to sew. Some wore necklaces made of shells and animals' teeth.

Weapons, tools and ornaments

Pointed hand-axe showing how we think it was held and used

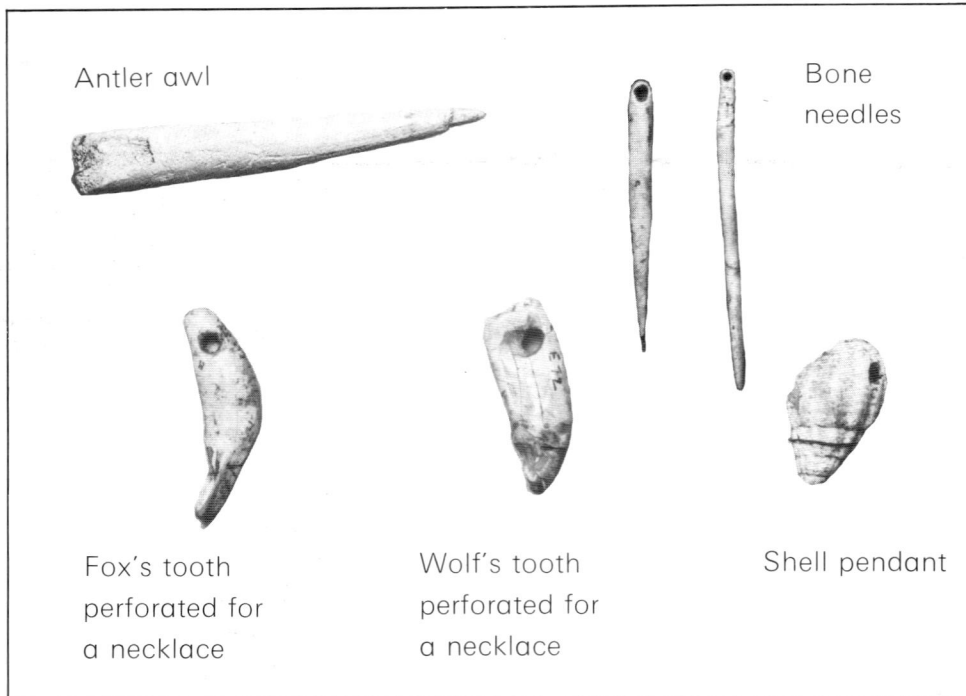

Antler awl

Bone needles

Fox's tooth perforated for a necklace

Wolf's tooth perforated for a necklace

Shell pendant

Flint points. They probably had wooden handles and were used as knives for piercing and cutting.

Most wooden tools and weapons have rotted away, but this yew-wood spear was found at Clacton-on-Sea. It is probably the oldest wooden weapon.

Cave paintings

Men hunting

In some places, particularly in France and Spain, some Old Stone Age men painted pictures on the walls and roofs of their caves. Many of the paintings were of the animals they hunted – wild oxen, deer, bison, bears, horses and mammoths. Others were of men and women hunting and gathering food.

Look carefully at the pictures on this page and the next.
   The hunters believed that the paintings gave them magic power over their enemies and the animals they hunted. They painted their pictures deep inside the dark caves, far back from the entrance. Some were at the end of long narrow tunnels.
   The artists worked by the light of burning fat in stone lamps. Their paintings remained undiscovered for thousands of years.

Collecting honey in a bag. Notice the angry bees buzzing around.

Here is a painting of a bison in a cave in Altamira in Spain. It was discovered just about a hundred years ago and it is probably 10,000 years old.

The artists first scratched the picture on the rock, or drew it with a piece of charcoal or burnt wood. Then they often cut away the rock around the picture of the animal.

They made paint from lumps of red, brown and yellow rock. They ground them to a powder with pebbles on flat pieces of stone. They made black powder from burnt bones and soot.

They either blew the coloured powder on to the picture through pieces of hollow bone, or else mixed it up with animal fat to make a kind of paint. This they put on with their fingers or a brush made from pieces of hair or fur.

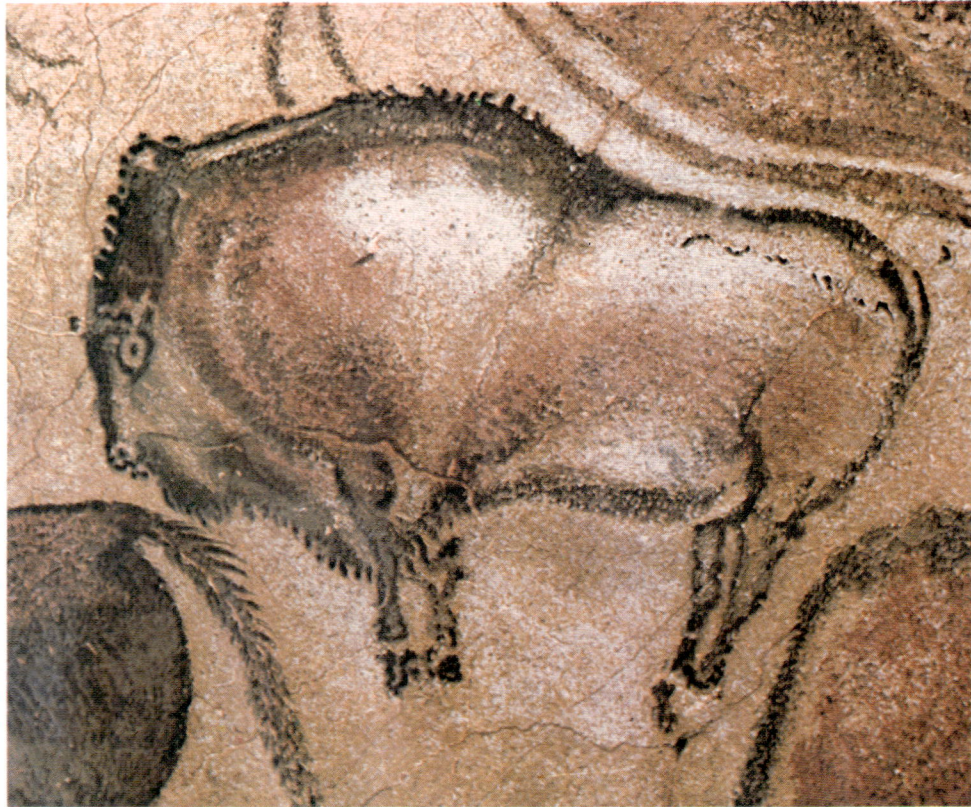

Cave painting of bison at Altamira, Spain

Things to do

1 Make a frieze for your classroom wall, showing what some of the first men looked like and how they lived.

2 Start to make your own book about the early men. Call the first chapter The Old Stone Age. Draw pictures and write notes about:
a) how the early men found their food
b) their homes
c) their tools and weapons.

3 Make models of some of the animals hunted by the early men. First, twist a piece of wire into the shapes of the animals and then wrap several layers of pasted newspaper tightly round the wire frames. When your animals are dry, paint them and stand them in front of your classroom frieze. Don't forget to label them.

4 Make a model of the entrance to a cave and show an early Stone Age family outside. Some of the hunters have returned from a hunt.

5 Look in other books in your school for pictures of cave paintings. Draw one of them in your book and write how they were made by the early Stone Age people.

The Middle Stone Age

Hunters and fishers

This picture shows a fen off the Norfolk coast with some hunters and fishers.

Look for:

—the fisherman with his catch of fish and the spears and harpoons he has used to catch them

—the other fisherman spearing for fish from his dug-out canoe. How do you think he made it?

—the two men carrying a dead animal hanging from a pole. The hunters shot deer, wild pig and wild oxen with their bows and arrows.

—the skin being pegged out on the ground to dry.

By this time, about 10,000 years ago, the climate began to change. The weather became warmer. The animals and plants changed. Forests spread over the grasslands, so the large herds of reindeer, bison and mammoths moved away. Red deer, pigs and bears took their place.

Men changed their ways, too. Groups of people came to Britain from Europe. They were hunter-fishers. We call this time the Middle Stone Age.

marshy fen

BRITAIN

EUROPE

Britain was still joined to Europe, but by a marshy fen.

A Middle Stone Age family

The picture above shows a hunting camp made by some hunter-fishers at Star Carr, near Scarborough, in Yorkshire. They used it when hunting in the winter and spring time. The hunter-fishers lived in forest lands and by the side of lakes, rivers and the seashore. At that time this part of Britain between the forest and the sea was damp, marshy fenland.

The camp was built on the marshy ground at the edge of a large lake. It was a platform made of birch tree branches and brushwood. Pebbles and lumps of clay held it down. We think the families lived on it in tents made of skins or of twigs and reeds.

right: These rolls of birch bark were found on the brushwood flooring at Star Carr. Strips of bark were cut from the trunks of trees and stored in rolls. They were used for flooring and for making containers. The Star Carr people did not know how to make pottery.

Weapons, tools and ornaments

The Middle Stone Age people hunted and trapped small animals and birds. For this they used bows and arrows, with tiny sharp flints as arrow-heads.

They fished with spears, bone hooks and nets. They made better axes to cut down trees in the forests. Some of their weapons had wooden shafts or handles.

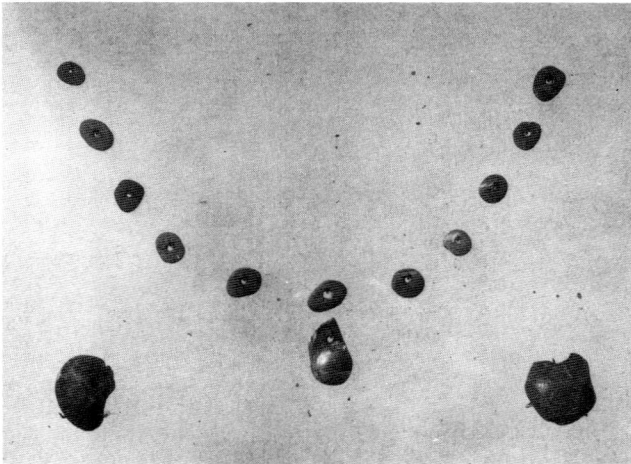

These beads and pendants were found at Star Carr. The beads were made of shale pebbles. Two of the pendants below them were carved from amber and the other from a stag's tooth.

These barbed heads were found at Star Carr. They were made from stags' antlers and were used for catching fish.

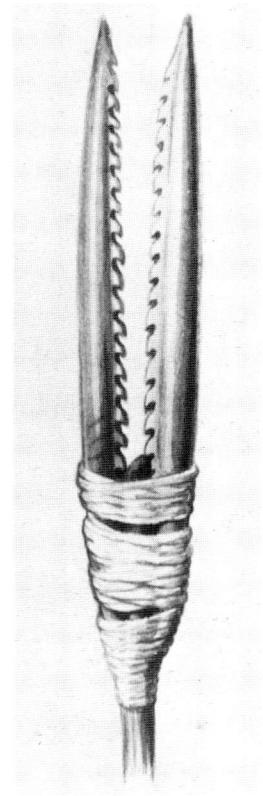

Some barbed heads were fastened together like this, for spearing fish.

Things to do

1 In your book start another chapter called The Middle Stone Age. Draw pictures and write notes about:
a) hunters and fishers
b) lakeside villages
c) weapons, tools and ornaments.

2 Paint a large picture of a Middle Stone Age lakeside camp. Show some of the men spearing fish from their dug-out canoe and others hunting wild animals with their bows and arrows.

3 Imagine you lived in the Middle Stone Age. Write a story in your book about all the things you did in one day. Perhaps you helped to clean and cook the fish your father caught, or to dry out the animal skins. Remember the tools you would have used.

The New Stone Age
Farmers and crops

About 11,000 years ago men living in a part of the world now called the Middle East began to tame and breed wild cattle, sheep and goats. They also discovered that wheat and barley, which grew wild there, could be sown and harvested for food. These men were the first farmers.

As time passed, these ways of farming spread into Europe. About 6,000 years ago some early farmers moved into Britain, bringing with them seed corn, cattle, sheep and pigs. They settled first in southern England. As well as breeding cattle they also began to clear plots of land and grow crops. This time in our story is called the New Stone Age.

What is happening in the picture?

Find:
—the men chopping down trees and burning branches
—the men and women breaking up the soil with digging sticks and stone hoes
—the basket of corn seed.

The picture shows how the men and women prepared a plot of land for sowing the corn. In time the crops used up the goodness in the soil and the farmers had to clear new plots.

Men still had to hunt and fish for food. But now they were farmers, they became more settled instead of moving from place to place. They began to live in villages.

Antler pick, ox-shoulder shovel and rake

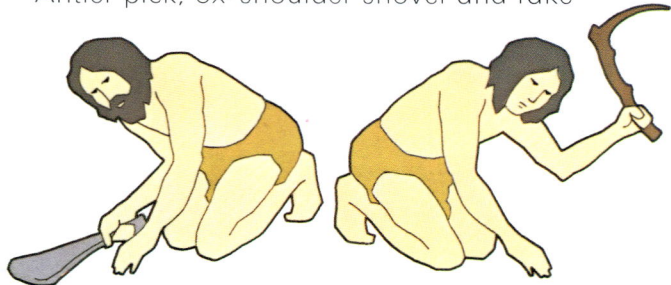

Digging stick

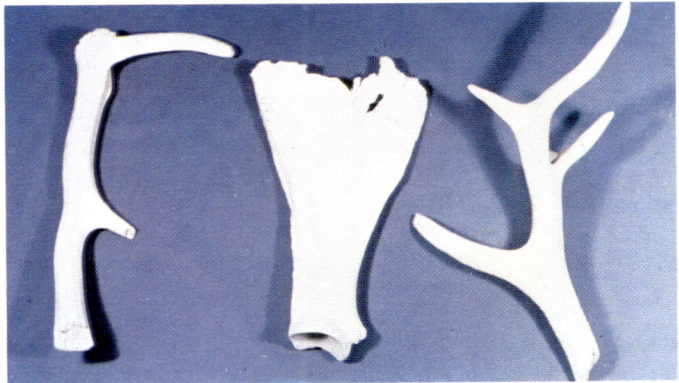

Flint sickle

Digging sticks, flint hoes and antler picks were used to break up the soil.

Then the seed was thrown over the ground and raked in with tree branches.

Stone quern used to grind corn into flour

Flint mining

Many of the tools and weapons were still made of flint. Good axes were needed to cut down trees. To get the best flint, New Stone Age men had to dig mines into chalk-land. There were flint mines at Grimes Graves in Norfolk, Cissbury in Sussex and at other places on the South Downs and near Salisbury.

This picture shows men working in one of the flint mines at Grimes Graves.

Look for:
—the mine shaft which was dug down to reach the best flint, called floorstone
—the tree trunk across the top of the shaft
—the ladder which led to the bottom of the shaft
—the man pulling the leather bag of flints to the top by a rope
—the passageways, or galleries, at the bottom of the shaft
—the three men digging flint in the galleries.

After the flint reached the top of the mine it was passed to the axe-makers. New Stone Age axes were better than those made earlier. They were rubbed and polished on a stone slab. This gave them a sharp edge. They were then taken by traders to different parts of the country and exchanged for other goods.

In the north and west of England polished axe-heads were made from rocks which were harder than flint. These again were traded to other parts of the country, even into the flint mining areas.

Weapons and tools

Here are some of the weapons and tools used during the New Stone Age.

This flint axe has been fastened into a wooden handle.

A flint axe and rubbing stone. The axes were chipped to a sharp edge and then polished on the wetted stone.

This man is felling a tree with a New Stone Age flint axe.

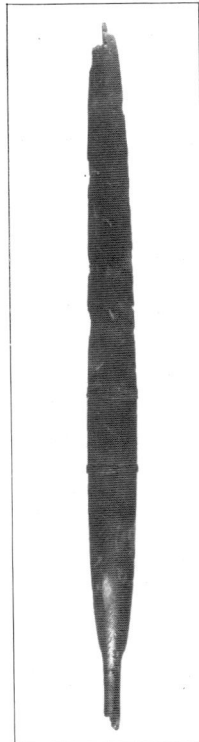

Flint arrow-heads

Men still hunted animals and birds and fished for food.

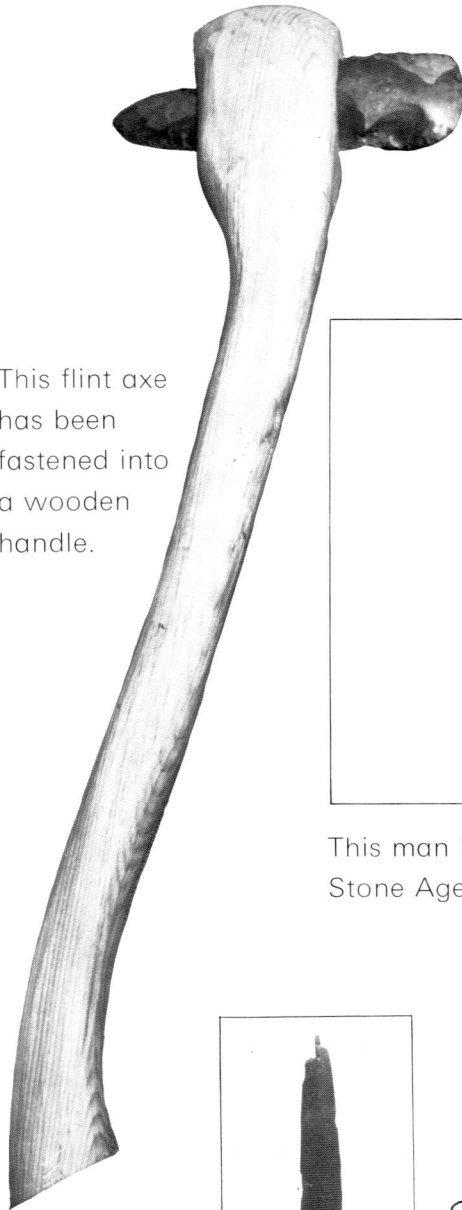

Part of a longbow of yew and a drawing to show how it fired an arrow with a flint arrow-head

Clothes, ornaments and containers

Here is a picture of a family of the New Stone Age – father, mother, daughter and young son. Notice what each person is wearing in the picture. What is the young boy doing in the family picture?

Although spinning and weaving was being carried out in other parts of Europe, New Stone Age people in Britain were still wearing clothes made from skins of the animals they kept.

People in the New Stone Age used various types of containers. They made baskets, leather bags, stone bowls and clay pots for holding foods and liquids.

left: Pottery bowl

right: Bag-shaped pot, probably copied from a leather bag

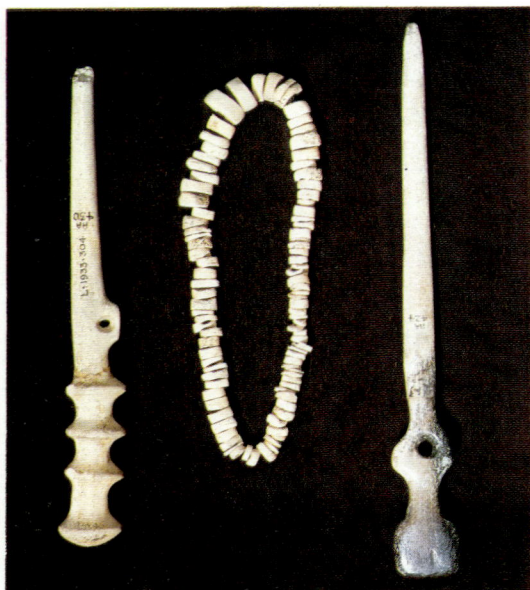

left: Bone and ivory ornaments found at Skara Brae in the Orkneys. The pins were used for fastening clothes.

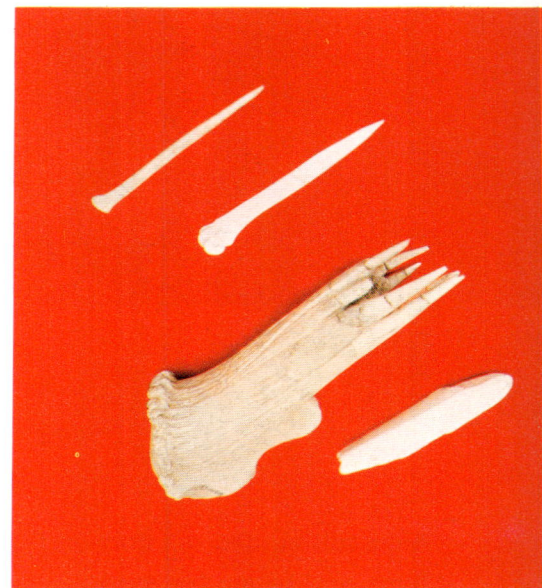

right: Leather-working tools from Windmill Hill. The comb removed rough hair. The gouge cleaned the skin and the points made holes for sewing, or were used as costume pins.

Homes

We do not know much about the kind of houses the early farmers lived in. The remains of a rectangular house have been found at Haldon in Devon. This picture shows what it may have looked like.

Below it is another New Stone Age house which was built in Ireland. Round houses like this may have been built in England.

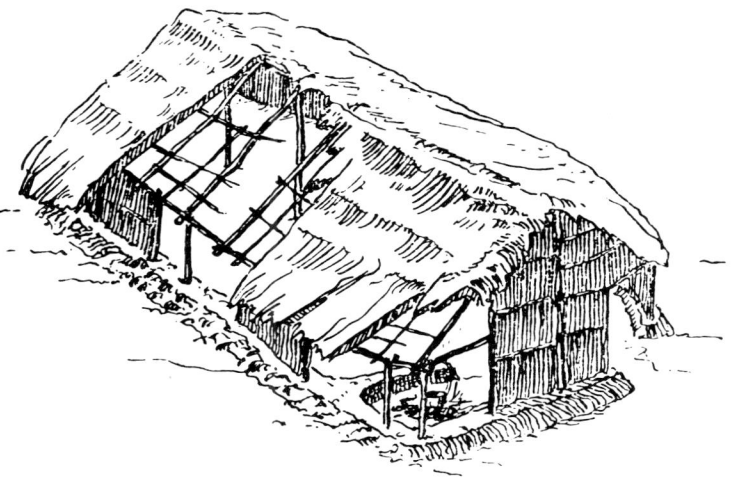

Causewayed camps

In the south of England the remains of huge camps have been found, usually on high ground. Look at the picture below of one of these camps at Windmill Hill, near Avebury, in Wiltshire. The photograph was taken from an aeroplane.

Find:
— the pits or ditches
— the circular banks or slopes round the camp
— the gaps between the pits. These were paths, or causeways, from one slope to another.

Experts now think these camps were used as meeting places – for the worship of gods and for holding feasts – and perhaps as market places to exchange things such as cattle and food.

Long barrows

New Stone Age people buried some of their dead under large mounds of earth or chalk rubble. The mounds were often between 30 and 45 metres long and some were even 90 metres long. The end where the bodies were buried was usually 2 metres or more high and the other end sloped down to the ground. These burial mounds were called long barrows and were built by the early farmers.

The picture above shows one kind of barrow, called a timbered long barrow.

Find:
—the long timber palisade, or fencing
—the wooden buildings like houses inside the palisade
—the men covering the buildings with the mound of earth. How did they move the earth from the ditches which ran along each side of the mound?

Not everyone was buried in mounds like these. Probably only important people and their families were buried there.

The bodies were not all buried at the same time. In this type of barrow they were stored in timber or turf 'houses' until it was decided to build the mound over the houses. After this, no more bodies could be put inside.

These four skeletons were discovered buried in a long barrow. The skeleton in the centre is of a child about 12 years old. The other three are men.

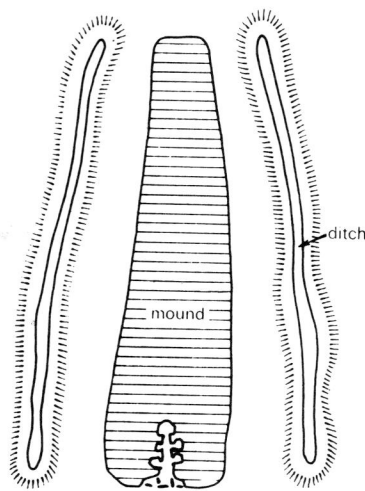

above: Plan of West Kennet long barrow

Inside West Kennet long barrow

Other burial places called chambered barrows were built by people who came to England from France after the early farmers.

On the left is a picture taken from the air of the barrow at West Kennet in Wiltshire. Find the entrance at the end of the barrow. This led into a short stone-built passage. At the far end of the passage, and on each side of it, were tiny rooms, or chambers, where the dead bodies were placed. The entrance was sealed with large stones until it was opened again for more bodies to be placed inside.

When it was decided to close the tomb, the chamber and passage were filled with rubble and the entrance was sealed off with huge stones.

Things to do

1 Make a chapter for your book about the New Stone Age. Draw pictures and write notes about:
a) early farmers working in their fields and using some of their tools
b) flint mining
c) long barrows.
2 Make models on a table in your classroom of: a) a New Stone Age village, or b) a flint mine, or c) a chambered long barrow.

3 Make a wall frieze for your classroom of a) early farmers clearing the land and starting to grow crops, or b) mining for flint, or c) closing and covering a long barrow.
4 Try to visit museums in your district and look for weapons and tools of the New Stone Age. Make drawings and write notes about them for your own book.
5 Find out more about the New Stone Age people from other books in your school or public library.

The Bronze Age
Bronze-smiths

About 4,000 years ago more people crossed the sea to Britain from Europe. They conquered the lands of the New Stone Age farmers. We call these people the Beaker Folk because of the shape of their pots.

These people still used stone and flint tools. But they also brought some tools made of metal and they bought more from metal-smiths in Ireland and Scotland.

At first the metal-smiths made the new tools from copper. Then they mixed tin with the copper to make bronze. Bronze tools were harder, stronger and had better cutting edges. This time in our history is called the Bronze Age.

A Bronze Age beaker

The picture above shows travelling bronze-smiths at work.
Find:
—the boy using the bellows at the fire
—the cup on the fire. The fire melted the copper and bronze
—the man pouring the hot molten metal into the mould to make an axe-head. When the metal cooled, the axe was taken from the mould.
—the second man hammering and sharpening an axe already taken from the mould.

Bronze spear head, dagger and pin, with a stone battle axe

A cauldron made from bronze plates rivetted together

A bucket made from sheet bronze. It is about $\frac{1}{2}$ metre high.

Sword of later Bronze Age. These later swords were used for slashing, rather than stabbing.

A trumpet found at County Antrim in Ireland

Bronze shields like this one were probably used at important ceremonies.

At first only a few things were made of bronze, but as time passed copper and tin became more plentiful. Other groups of people came to Britain and some had their own bronze-smiths. New ways of making tools were discovered, so more and better bronze tools were made.

Some of the bronze-smiths worked for the chiefs and important warriors. But others travelled round the countryside, making and selling new tools and weapons in exchange for old, broken tools, food and any other things they needed.

Later, the smiths discovered how to beat bronze into sheets. Then they rivetted the sheets together to make beautiful shields, cauldrons and buckets. Sometimes they made musical wind instruments for the wealthy chieftains and their families. But flint and wooden tools and weapons were still used.

Farming

For a long time in the Bronze Age the tribesmen were mainly herdsmen. They moved from place to place, looking for fresh grasslands for their herds and flocks of cattle and sheep. They may have lived in tents. Or they dug shallow holes in the ground and over them built small huts made of mud and twigs.

About 3,000 years ago groups of Celts began to come over from Germany and France. These people were more interested in growing crops.

Here is a picture of a farm found at Itford Hill, in Sussex.

Find:
—the round wooden huts with thatched roofs and entrance porches. Some were living huts for about 20 people. Others were cattle barns and workshops. One was a weaving shed. Another hut was used for cooking.
—the fences round the huts and the gates
—the ponds inside the fences. What were they used for?
—the square cornfields. How many are there?
—the man with the plough pulled by two oxen
—the flock of sheep and the shepherd
—the cattle or oxen
—the hunter and his dog.

These farmers brought with them ploughs pulled by oxen. These ploughs did not turn the soil over as modern ploughs do. They only scratched the surface with the short, sharp point.

Corn was cut with sickles, dried, threshed and then stored for use later.

An early Bronze Age pot found in Yorkshire. The decoration was probably done with finger nails while the clay was soft.

Sickle blade

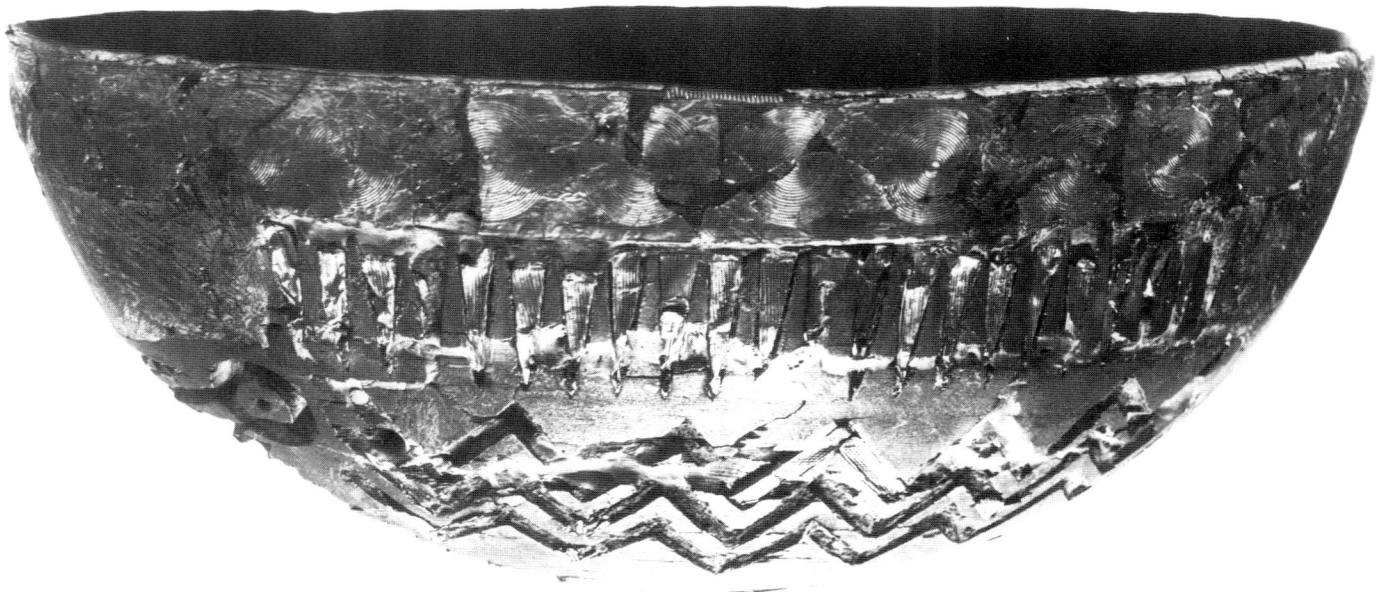

This is known as the 'ship bowl'. Look for the round shields, the triangular oars and the zig-zag waves of the sea.

Clothes, ornaments and jewellery

Here is a picture of a Bronze Age family. Notice that women have now learned how to spin and weave and make clothes.

Men wore cloaks, probably over tunics with shoulder straps. The cloaks were fastened with buttons, or long pins. Their belts were fastened with jet rings.

Women probably wore a skirt and jacket. Their hair was kept in place with pins and tied with string.

Some of the tribesmen were traders, passing ornaments and jewellery from the gold and bronze-smiths in Ireland to customers in Britain and Europe. They brought back amber ornaments from lands across the North Sea.

The chieftains and their families became rich from this trading and were able to buy precious ornaments, like those shown here.

This picture shows how many women may have worn Bronze Age jewellery and ornaments.

1 dress fastener
2 ear-rings
3 neck torc
4 armlet
5 bracelet
6 cuff fasteners

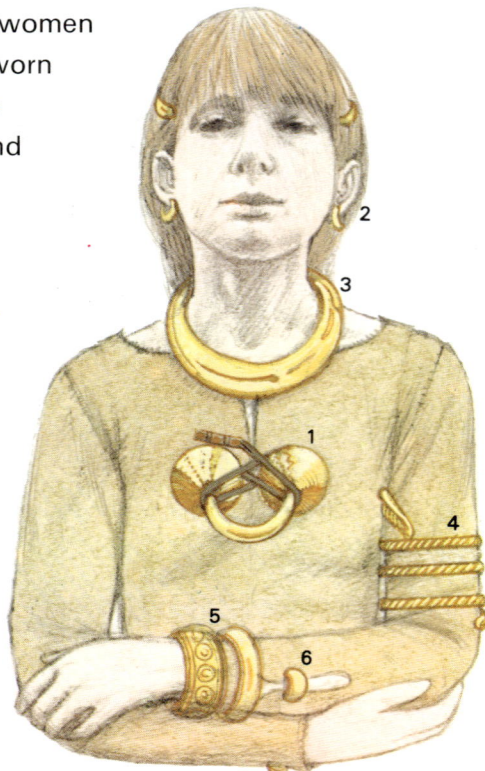

A jet necklace found at Melfort, Scotland

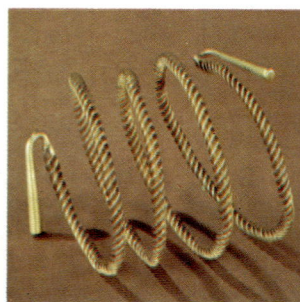

Ribbons of gold were twisted and made into armlets.

Neck ornaments like this were called lunulae. They were made from sheets of gold which were hammered flat, cut and decorated.

This cup was carved from a single piece of amber. It was found in a grave at Hove, in Sussex, with a bronze dagger and a stone battle-axe. Other cups were made from shale.

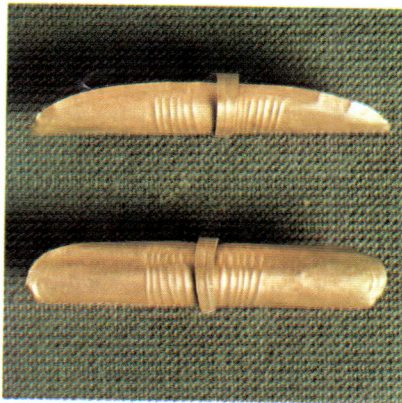

This cup was hammered out of a lump of gold. The thin gold has been 'corrugated' to make it stronger. The cup was found at Rillaton, in Cornwall.

Ear-rings, shaped like little baskets, were made from thin, beaten gold and bronze.

A torc or neck ornament, made of twisted gold bars

The cape on the left is the largest piece of gold work of the Bronze Age to be found. It was discovered near Mold, in North Wales, wrapped round the bones of a skeleton in a grave. The cape may have had a leather or cloth lining. The picture shows how it would have looked when it was worn.

Burials

For quite a long time in the Bronze Age, important people were buried under large round mounds of earth and stones, with a ditch round them. But the mounds contained only one body. These mounds are called round barrows. We can still see many of them today. This photograph of two round barrows in Sussex was taken from an aeroplane.

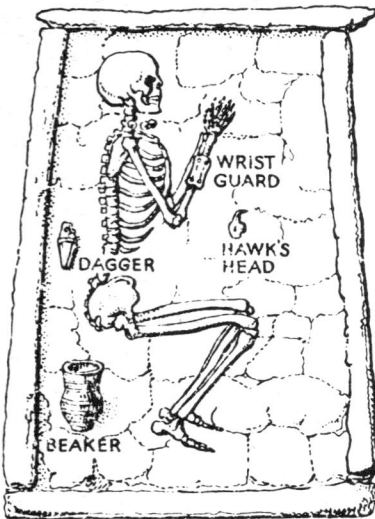

The picture on the left shows a skeleton of a Beaker warrior, or chieftain. The body was laid on its side, with its legs drawn up, in the way he used to sleep. It was protected by a box or 'cist', made of slabs of stone.

Later, dead bodies were cremated, or burned. The ashes were put in pots, called urns, and placed in the side of a round mound or buried in the ground in cemeteries.

A cremation urn

Temples

Some Bronze Age people built circles of large stone blocks like those shown on this page. These may have been temples where they worshipped their gods.

These pictures show how two of these temples may have looked. One was at Avebury and the other at Stonehenge.

above: Avebury   *below:* Stonehenge

Things to do

1 Chapter 4 of your book will be called The Bronze Age. Draw pictures and write notes about:

a) the bronze-smiths

b) tools and weapons

c) farming

d) clothes, ornaments and jewellery

e) temples.

2 Make a model of a Bronze Age farm and label what each of the huts was used for. You will find the picture on page 22 helpful.

3 Paint large pictures of:

a) bronze-smiths making weapons

b) Bronze Age farmers working on their land.

4 Make a model of Stonehenge.

5 Find out more about Bronze Age temples from books in your library. You will find something about them in the *Focus on History* book called *Stone Age to Iron Age.*

The Iron Age

About 2,500 years ago more Celtic warrior tribes continued to come to Britain from Europe. These warriors still used bronze, but they also brought with them swords and tools made from a new metal – iron.

Iron was harder than copper or bronze and made better tools. There was more of it, so in time more and more iron tools and weapons were made. More people could have good tools for their work and stronger weapons for fighting.

Iron tools were hammered into shape by smiths and not cast like bronze.

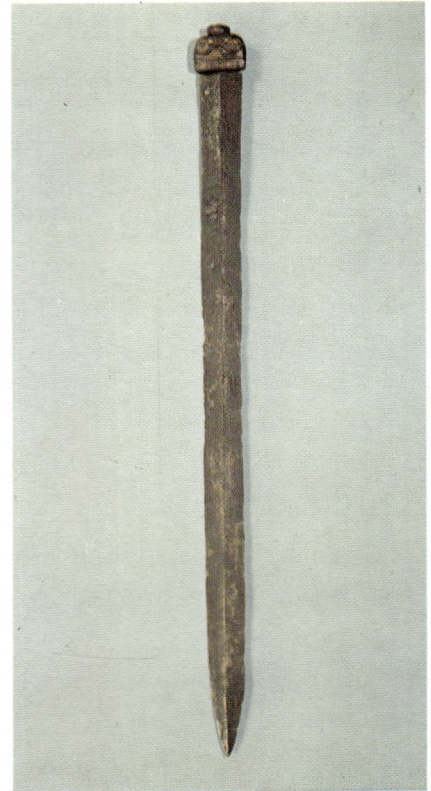

A sword with an iron blade

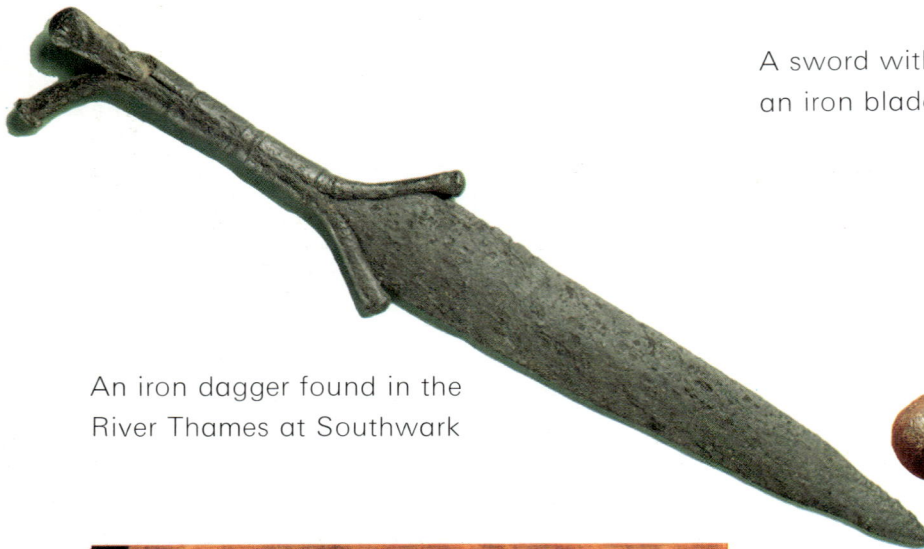

An iron dagger found in the River Thames at Southwark

An iron sickle and a billhook

A bronze hilt to an iron dagger

Farms and villages

The Iron Age farmers lived very much like those in the Bronze Age. They grew crops of wheat, oats and barley and kept herds of cattle and flocks of sheep.

The picture shows a model of part of an Iron Age farm which was at West Harling, in Norfolk. It can be seen in the Castle Museum at Norwich.

Notice:
—the round house. The farmer and his family lived in part of the house. The rest was used as a cattle shed and storehouse.
—the yard in the middle
—the gate into the yard
—the ditch and the raised paths, or causeways, over it.

Men hunted red deer, wild pigs, beavers and cranes. The skins were still cleaned with flint scrapers.

The women made their own pots, spun yarn and wove cloth on upright looms.

Above is another Iron Age
farm, which was at Little
Woodbury, in Wiltshire.
Find:
—the round farmhouse for the
 farmer and his family
—the fence round the
 farmhouse. Outside the
 fence was a ditch
—the animals.
You can find out more about
this farm in the *Focus on
History* book *Stone Age to
Iron Age.*

This was an Iron Age village at Glastonbury, in Somerset.
It was built in marshland. The huts were built on a platform
made of logs and brushwood.

Here are some of the tools used during the Iron Age.

A pair of bridle-bits for horses

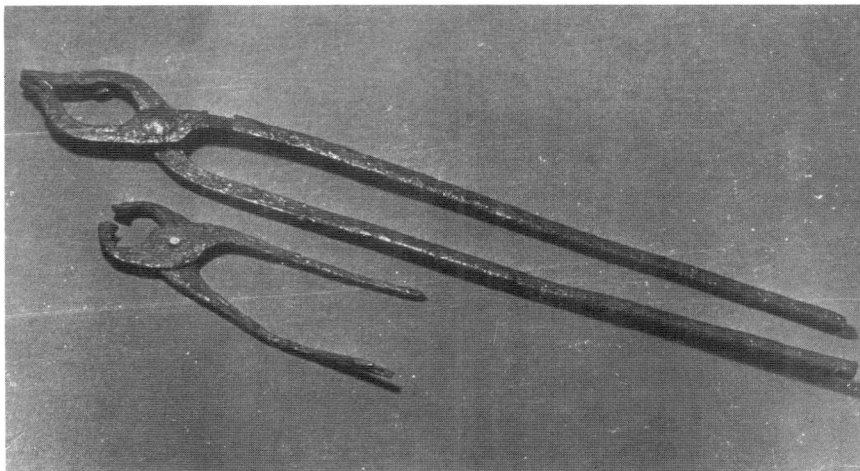

Blacksmith's tongs

Iron Age 'fire-dogs'. The ends have been made in the shape of ox heads.

above: An Iron Age rotary quern used for grinding corn into flour.

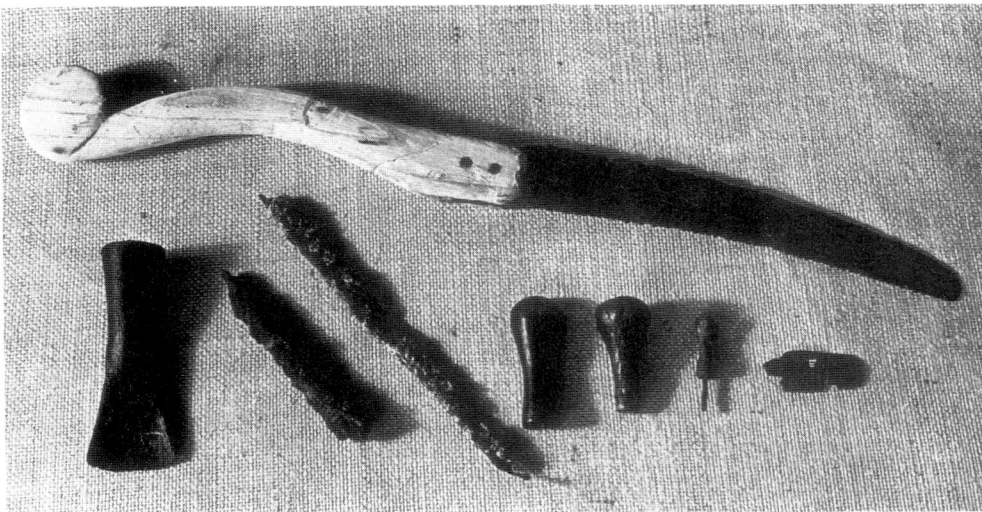

Carpentry tools: a large wooden-handled saw, a gouge, two files, an awl and awl handles and a small saw

Clothes, ornaments and other objects

Here is a picture of an Iron
Age family. They liked brightly
coloured clothes and jewellery.

A model of a loom for
weaving clothes. It can be
seen in Norwich Museum.

A poor man's iron
collar and parts of
necklaces of tusks,
teeth and beads

These gold torcs were
discovered at Ipswich.

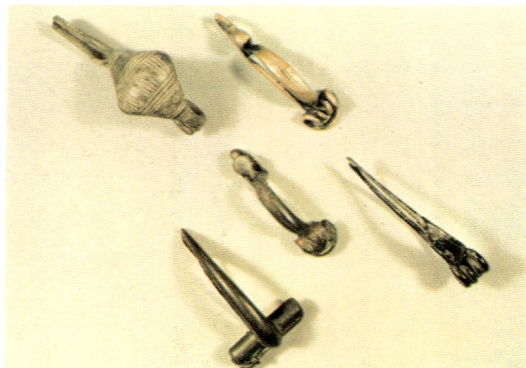

Iron Age brooches used to
fasten clothing, especially the
cloak at the neck

A wooden bucket
with bronze decoration.

These two pages show some things from the Iron Age that can be seen in museums.

Though iron was used, many objects were made from bronze and gold, and flint was still used, too.

Look carefully at the patterns made by the fine craftsmen.

It is unlikely this bronze helmet was used in battle as it was not strong enough. It was probably worn on special occasions.

A wooden tankard covered over with sheet bronze

Iron Age pottery bowl. Some pots were now made on a potter's wheel.

right: A bronze mirror with a beautifully patterned back. The front was polished to make it reflect the face.

above: This bronze shield was found in the River Witham in Lincolnshire.

33

Hill forts

This photograph was taken from an aeroplane. It shows an old Iron Age hill fort at Beacon Hill, in Hampshire.

Notice:

—it is on the top of high ground

—the banks and ditches round the fort to protect it from attackers. At first there would be only one line of ditch and bank. But when slings were used to hurl stones, more banks and ditches had to be dug to keep the slingers further away.

—the entrance to the fort. This had to be made as strong as possible and difficult for any attackers to enter.

Many forts like this were built on hills during the Iron Age. The hill forts were meeting places for the tribe and places where the tribesmen took their families, cattle and sheep, in times of danger.

Some forts were perhaps the homes of the tribes' chiefs and their families and followers. Others were like small towns, with streets of round houses with thatched roofs, temples where the tribal gods were worshipped and workshops for the craftsmen.

Britain was divided amongst several tribes by the end of the Iron Age. Some of these tribes were the Belgae. They had come from Gaul (now France) to escape from the Roman army and its general, Julius Caesar. Caesar was then conquering Gaul for the Romans.

The Belgae were good farmers. They began to clear the trees in the forest lands. Then they cultivated the soil with their iron-tipped ploughs.

The Belgae chiefs or kings were powerful. Some minted their own gold, silver and copper coins. They traded corn, cattle, hunting dogs, leather and slaves, for Roman wine, pottery, glass and silver tableware from Gaul.

Things to do

1 Start a new chapter called The Iron Age. Draw pictures and write notes about:
a) tools and weapons
b) clothes, ornaments and jewellery
c) hill forts.
2 Make models of:
a) Glastonbury Iron Age village
b) an Iron Age farmhouse.
3 Write in your book the story of an attack on a hill fort and draw a picture about your story.
4 Look at the curved patterns on the mirror on page 33. Make up your own patterns of curves like these and colour them.
5 Make a wall frieze of the ornaments and jewellery worn during the Iron Age.
6 Imagine you lived on a farm during the Iron Age. Write down all the things you did on the farm during one day.

An attack on a hill fort

Roman Britain
The Roman army

At this time in our history, the Roman army was the finest in the world. It had two main kinds of regiments – the legions and the auxilia.

A legion had 5,000 to 6,000 soldiers, called legionaries. These men were infantry (soldiers who fought on foot). They usually signed on in the army for 20 to 25 years.

Each legion was divided into companies of 80 men, called centuries. As well as being first-class fighting men, the legionaries were skilled engineers and craftsmen. They could build roads, forts and bridges. When they were not fighting they lived in fortresses, ready for any danger or sudden emergency.

The picture on the right shows a legionary. Find:
—his long throwing spear, or javelin
—his short, stabbing sword
—his shield
—the hilt, or handle, of his dagger (just above the top of his shield)
—his helmet
—his tunic and armour
—his sandals, fastened round his ankles.

left: A centurion was in charge of a century.

right: A standard-bearer led his legion into battle. His hood was made of bear and leopard skin.

The soldiers in the auxilia came from tribes which the Romans had conquered. Their job was to help the legions. In battle they fought in front of, and at the sides of, the legions, protecting them from any sudden attack from the enemy.

After the Romans conquered Britain, the auxiliaries guarded the forts on the frontier, or boundary line, against enemy tribes.

The auxiliaries were divided into cohorts, or wings, of 500 or 1,000 men. Some were infantry soldiers. Others fought on horseback and some were archers and stone-slingers.

Here is a foot-soldier from the auxiliaries. Find his spear, sword, dagger and shield. How is his armour different from that of the legionary on the opposite page? What is the difference between his shield and the shield of the legionary?

The picture below was carved in stone. The soldier's friends had it made in memory of him when he died. It shows an auxiliary cavalryman who fought on horseback. He is riding over the body of a Briton.

An auxiliary foot-soldier

The words at the bottom of the tombstone tell us that he was 40 (XL) years old and that he fought for the Romans for 22 (XXII) years.

The Roman armies come to Britain

This map shows the Roman Empire. The empire had started from the city of Rome. Over a long time its soldiers conquered all the lands which are shaded on the map. Rome was then the centre of a huge empire.

In 55 B.C. (that is 55 years before the birth of Jesus Christ) and again in the following year, the famous Roman general, Julius Caesar, brought his army to Britain.

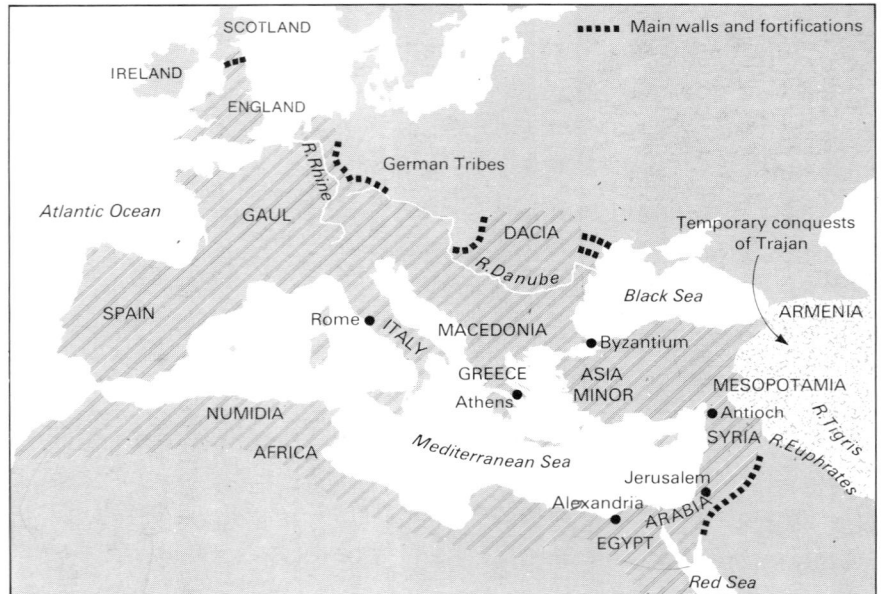

Some of the Belgic tribes in Britain were helping Caesar's enemies in Gaul (now France) and some of his enemies had escaped to Britain. Caesar had also heard that Britain was a rich country and it might be worth conquering it.

So he crossed the English Channel from France with his army to find out about Britain for himself. He drove back the Belgic tribes who were waiting for him. But on both visits storms damaged his ships and so he went back to Gaul. The Roman army did not return to Britain until 90 years later.

Julius Caesar

Belgic warriors and chariots

In A.D. 43 the Roman Emperor, Claudius, decided to conquer Britain and make it a part of the Roman Empire. He sent about 40,000 troops. They landed at Richborough in Kent and won a battle at the River Medway. Claudius then came from Rome to join his army. Some of the tribes surrendered to him at Camulodunum (now Colchester) and then he returned to Rome.

The army continued to march north and west, gradually conquering most of the country. On their way they built new roads, bridges and forts, so they could move quickly and safely from place to place.

About A.D. 61, the tribe of the Iceni, under Queen Boudicca, with the Trinovantes, rebelled against the Romans. They set on fire the new Roman towns at Colchester, St. Albans and London. But the Romans defeated them and Boudicca killed herself with poison.

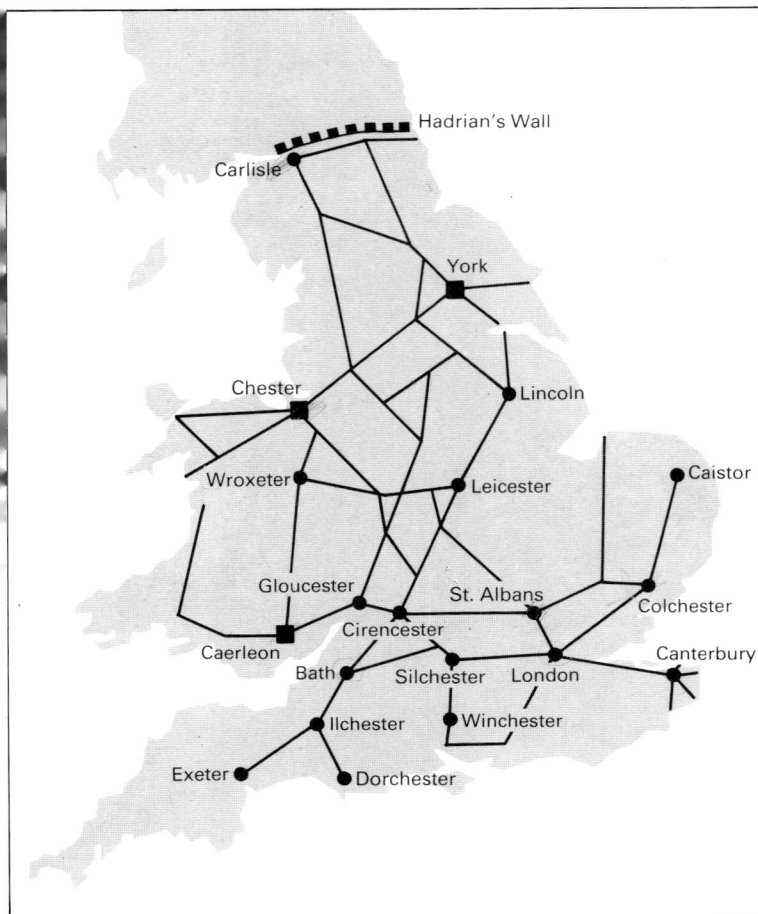

Claudius

In time the Romans conquered most of Britain, except the north of Scotland. The country became peaceful.

The Romans were good rulers. They built many new towns in the Roman way. They allowed the tribes to keep their own customs and gods. But they encouraged them, particularly the chiefs and important tribesmen, to dress, eat and live like Romans.

This map shows some of the roads, forts and towns built by the Romans.

The legionaries built strong fortresses and forts for the army. Their main fortresses were at York, Chester and Caerleon. Each was the headquarters of a legion.

This picture shows the Roman fortress at Chester.

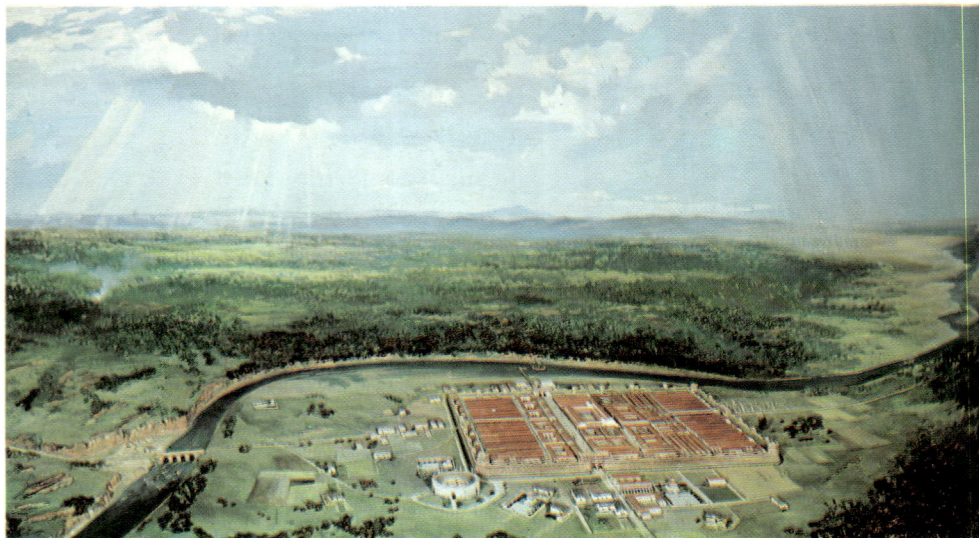

The Romans were the first people to build towns in Britain. Many of the towns had fine buildings, like this temple of Claudius at Colchester. It was set on fire by Boudicca's tribesmen.

You will find this model of the temple in the museum at Colchester.

Here is a model of a huge Roman palace. It was built at Fishbourne, in Sussex, about A.D. 75 – 80. Part of it can be seen today.

Perhaps it was built for Cogidubnus, the chief of the tribe of Regenses. He had helped the Romans in A.D. 43.

Hadrian's Wall

In A.D. 122 the Roman Emperor Hadrian came to Britain. He ordered the legions to build a great wall across the north of England, from sea to sea. It is still called Hadrian's Wall. It was 80 Roman miles (117 kilometres) long. The main parts were $4\frac{1}{2}$ metres high and $2\frac{1}{2}$ to 3 metres wide. The wall was the northern frontier, or boundary, of the Roman Empire.

It separated the tribes in Scotland from those in England. From it the Roman troops could go out and attack rebel tribes.

Seventeen forts were built along the wall. At every mile between the forts were smaller forts, called milecastles. Between the milecastles were signal turrets. All these were manned by regiments of the auxiliary soldiers.

Find the milecastle and the turret in the picture of the soldiers on the wall. To the south, behind the wall, was a deep, wide ditch, called the vallum.

above: Hadrian's Wall stretched from Bowness on the west coast to Wallsend on the east coast.

Part of the wall today

The picture above shows one of the forts on Hadrian's Wall. One thousand infantry soldiers lived and worked here.

Look for:
—the stone wall round the fort
—the main gateways
—part of Hadrian's Wall on each side of the fort.
—the village outside the fort.

On the right is a plan of the fort. Each building has a number. Use the plan to find these buildings in the top picture:
—the headquarters building. This had an open courtyard with a great hall along one side. Here, too, were the regiment's offices, a chapel and the strong-room for the soldiers' pay and savings.
—the commandant's house, where he lived with his family, servants and slaves
—the commandant's private bath-house
—the hospital, with rooms for patients and an operating theatre
—the granaries, for storing corn and other food supplies, such as olive oil, fish and dried meat
—the barrack blocks, where the soldiers lived.

Housesteads fort

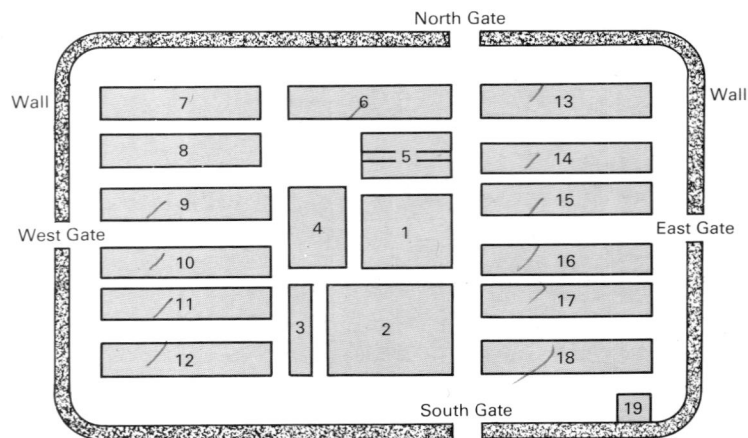

Plan of the fort

1 the headquarters building
2 the commandant's house
3 the commandant's bath-house
4 the hospital
5 the granaries
6 probably a stable or barn
7 to 18 most of these were barrack blocks, but number 10 may been a workshop.
19 the latrine, which was flushed from a water tank. The fort also had sewers.

The soldiers spent their time very much like our soldiers today. There was weapon training and drills, guard duties, route marches, battle practice and the cleaning of barracks and equipment.

They would spend their off-duty time in the bath-house, and in the shops, inns and houses in the village outside the fort. In the village lived the soldiers' wives and children, with merchants, craftsmen and farmers, who sold their goods to the soldiers, the village people and the tribesmen nearby.

Some of the soldiers married local girls. When they retired from the army, they stayed on in the village and their sons joined their father's regiment to be soldiers in the fort.

Things to do

1 Now make another book called Roman Britain. On the first page write the story of how the Romans came to Britain. Then draw pictures of some of the soldiers and write notes about them.

2 Paint large pictures to show:

a) the Roman soldiers landing on the shores of Britain and the Belgic tribes fighting them

b) Roman soldiers on Hadrian's Wall.

3 Make models of:

a) Hadrian's Wall

b) a Roman fort

c) a milecastle.

A milecastle

A granary for storing corn and food

The regiment's chapel with the statue of the emperor and the legion's standards

Clothes and jewellery

This picture shows a Roman family. Look at the clothes they are wearing.

Men wore short-sleeved tunics that reached to their knees. Important men wore a toga. This was a long piece of cloth, which they threw over their left shoulder and then wrapped round their body.

Women also wore tunics, sometimes embroidered, with a dress called a stola.

On their feet, both men and women wore leather slippers, sandals or boots.

Outdoors, they wore cloaks, sometimes with hoods. Poorer people wore only tunics. Children dressed like their parents.

Clothes were usually made of wool, but wealthy people sometimes wore linen, cotton or silk. The clothes were fastened with pins, brooches and buttons.

Well-to-do women liked jewellery. They wore rings, necklaces, ear-rings and bracelets.

They used make-up, or cosmetics, made from chalk, ashes and coloured earth. Perfume was bought from eastern countries.

A ring

A necklace and bracelet

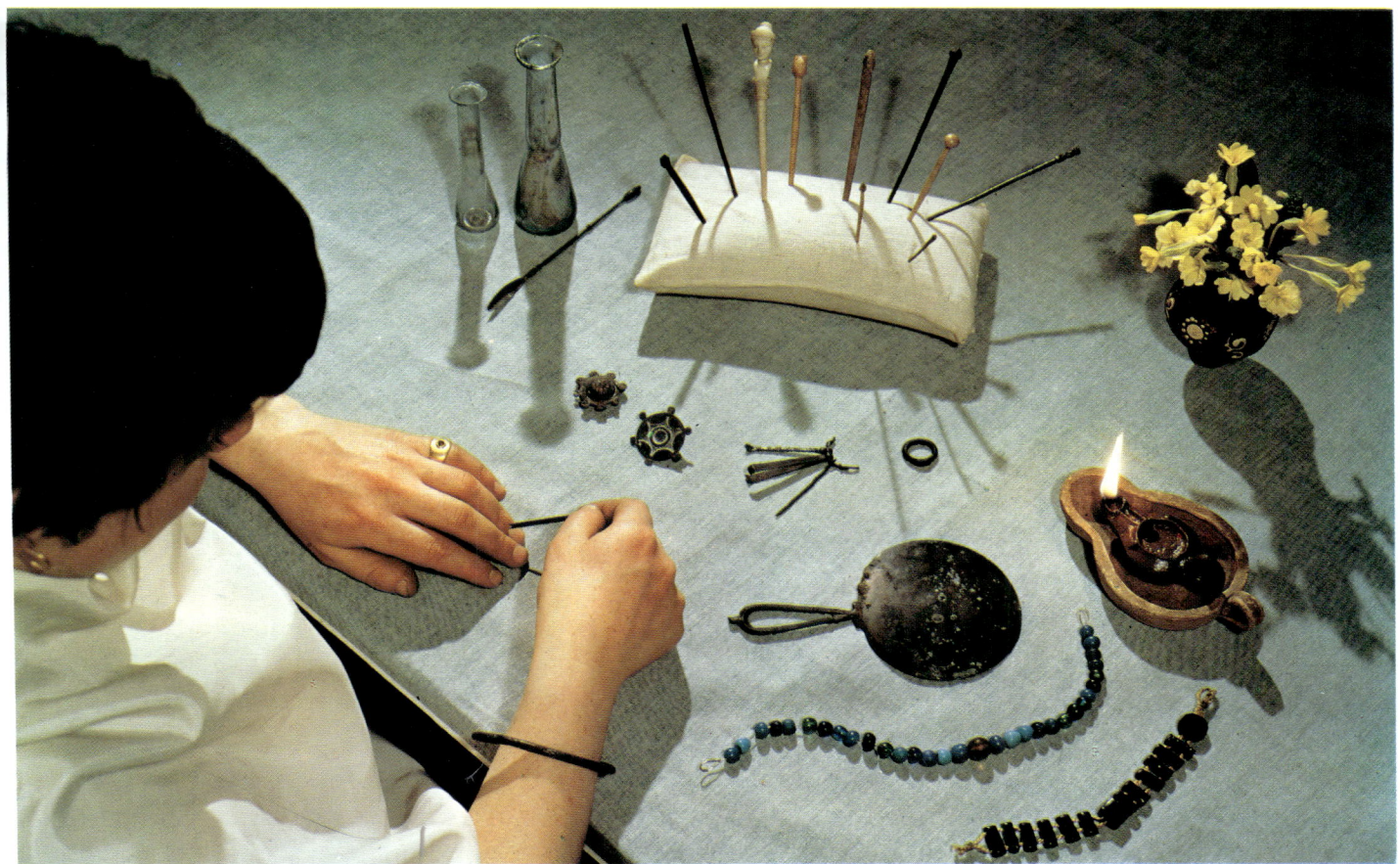

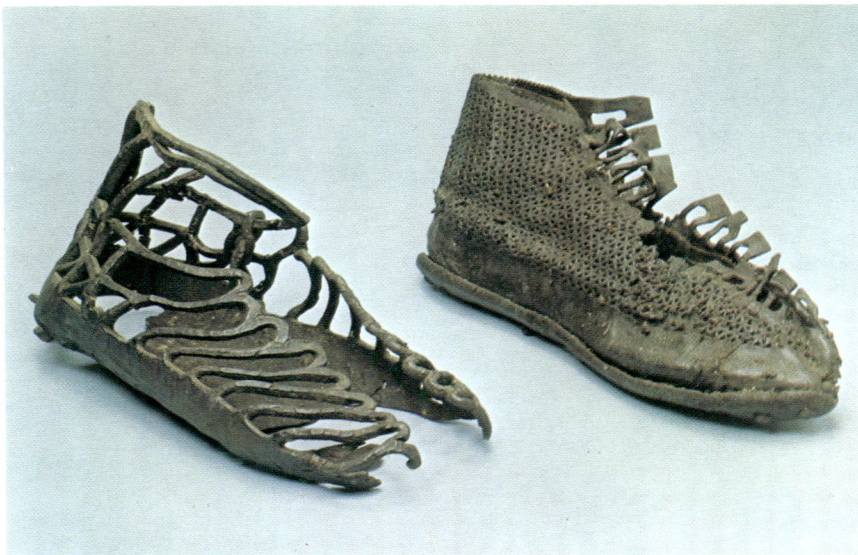

Look at the picture above of a lady's dressing-table.

Find:

—the small bottles that held cosmetics and perfume
—the bronze mirror
—the necklaces of beads
—her nail-cleaners
—her ring
—the bone hairpins.

Ladies also used combs, tweezers and ear-picks.

above: A shoe and a sandal   *below:* A jet necklace

Things to be found in museums

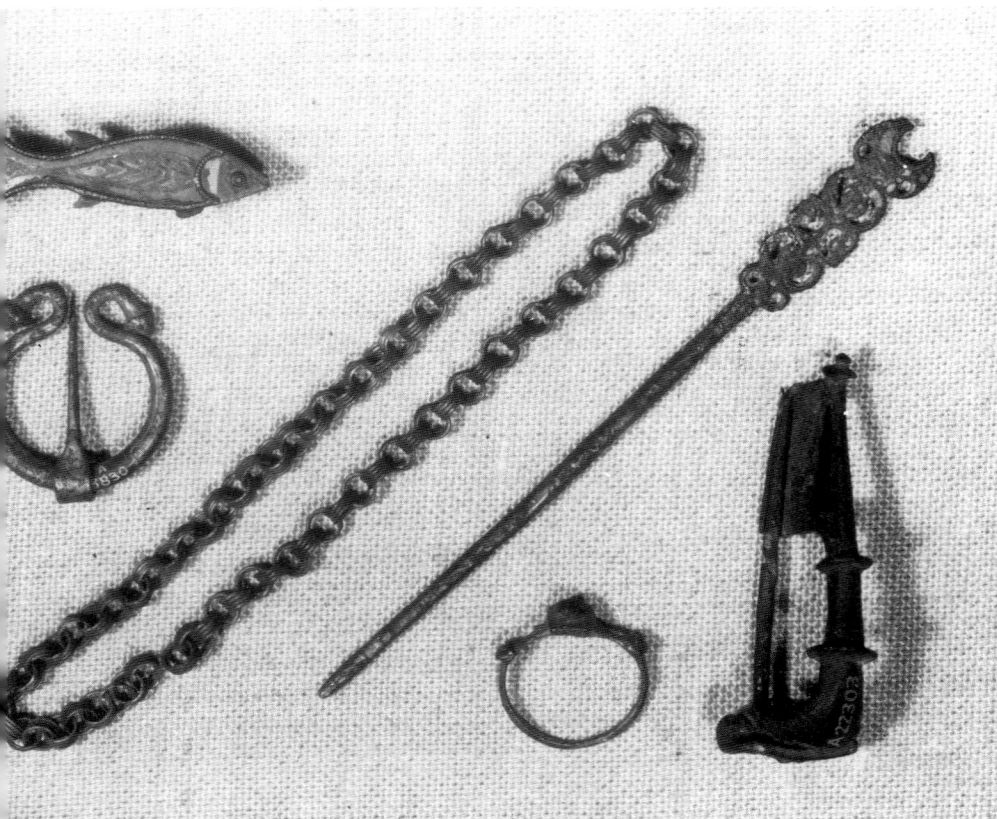

Visit your local museums and look for things used in Roman Britain. You may find some like those shown on these pages.

Here are:
—three brooches to fasten clothes
—a bracelet
—a hair-pin
—a ring.

The picture above shows a lady's hairstyle. Ladies liked elaborate hairstyles.

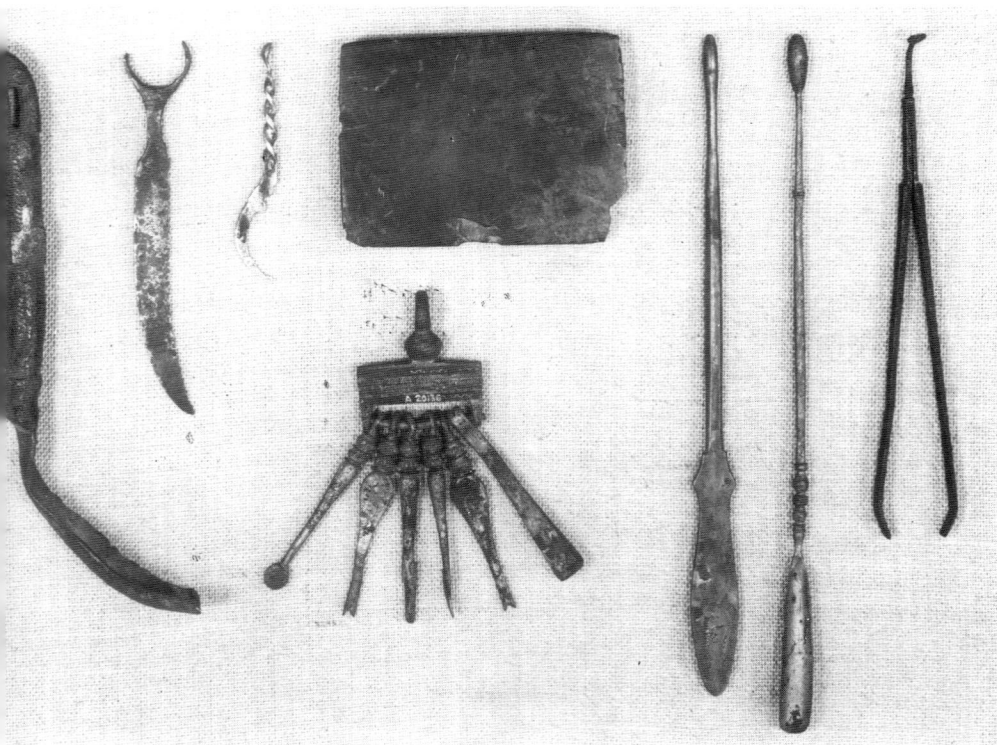

In this picture look for:
—the iron strigil, on the left, used in the baths to scrape off oil and dirt after massaging the skin
—next, the knife
—the small nail-cleaner
—the palette. Ladies mixed their cosmetics on it.
—the spatula for mixing the cosmetics
—the thin spoon for the cosmetic bottles
—the pair of tweezers
—the manicure set which was carried on a belt.

The Romans wrote messages, accounts and shopping lists on wax-covered wooden tablets. Look at the picture and find:
—the wooden tablets tied together
—the stylus on the tablets and the other one by the side. People wrote on the waxed tablets with the sharp point of the stylus. They used the flat blade at the other end to smooth out any mistakes.
—the inkwell. Sometimes letters were written on parchment with a pen.
—the oil lamp, beeswax, and seals. When the letters had been written, the tablets were tied with string. A blob of hot wax was dropped on the knot and the ring or seal was pressed on it. Why did they do this?

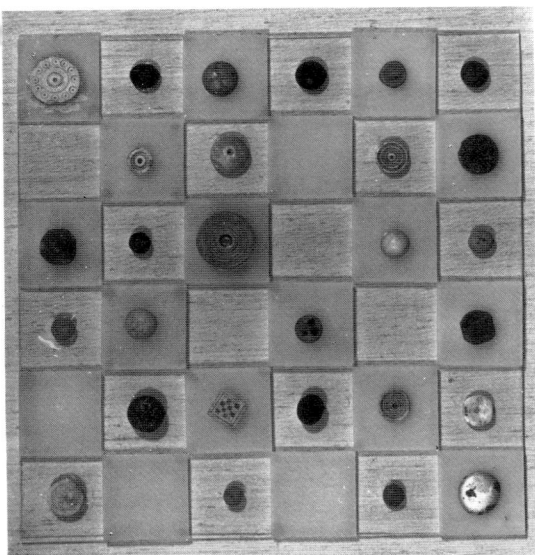

The Romans played a game like our draughts with stone, glass or lead discs on a stone board like this.

Another game was like 'five-stones' or 'knuckle-bones'. Five bones, or pieces of bronze or ivory, were thrown in the air and then caught on the back of the hand.

Children also played hopscotch.

Things to do

1 Draw pictures in your book of things used in Roman Britain which you have found in your local museums. Label them and write notes about them.
2 Make a wall picture of different kinds of Roman jewellery.

Towns in Roman Britain

The Romans built many new towns in Britain. These were planned like Roman towns.

Here is the Roman town of Verulamium (now St. Albans). See how the straight streets divided the town into blocks of land. On these were built fine Roman buildings – the town hall and market place, public baths and temples. There were also houses and shops. Round the town was a wall, at first built of earth and clay, but later in stone. There were also four main gates or entrances to the town.

In the centre of the towns was a group of buildings called the forum. Its courtyard was the town market place. Along one side was a large hall, called the basilica. This was the town hall and the court of justice, where the magistrates judged cases. Along the other three sides were shops and offices, and sometimes a temple.

Find the forum in the top picture of Verulamium.

Each town usually had several temples. Page 40 showed one at Colchester. Here is another at Verulamium. Services were held in the courtyard, where there was a statue of the goddess.

Look carefully at the houses and shops round the temple. Find also:
—the cart pulled by horses
—men carrying a litter
—men riding on horseback.

Find this temple in the picture of Verulamium on the opposite page. Look for the theatre shown in the next picture.

This is how the theatre at Verulamium may have looked. Find:
—the stage, where the actors performed their plays. Behind were the actors' dressing-rooms.
—the arena in front of the stage. There gladiators fought each other and acrobats did their acts.
—the rows of wooden seats, where 5,000 to 6,000 people could sit to watch the shows.

The model above of one of the main gates to the Roman town at Colchester can be seen in the museum there. Make a list of all the things you can find in the model.

Some towns and fortresses had an amphitheatre like the one on the right at Caerleon, in Wales.

People sat in rows of seats round the oval arena to watch:
—boxing and wrestling
—acrobats and jugglers
—gladiators
—bear baiting and cock fighting.

Along the street were rows of narrow shops with verandahs. The shops were open at the front, where the goods for sale were shown on counters. Behind the shops were workshops and living rooms.

People went to the public baths to meet their friends, to take exercise and to keep their bodies clean.

Important visitors to the town stayed at a large inn or hotel, called a mansio. The inn, like some of the larger houses, had its own baths.

left: Roman baths in London

Houses

The town houses were often long, narrow blocks of rooms. Some had extra rooms along the back.

The largest houses had rooms built around a courtyard. These rooms often had mosaic floors – patterns and pictures made with small pieces of coloured stones. They also had painted walls and ceilings.

Things to do

1 Make a wall picture to show a street in a town in Roman Britain. Remember to show the forum, a temple and shops.
2 Make models, or draw pictures, of a Roman theatre, an amphitheatre and the public baths.
3 Imagine you are living in Roman Britain.

Write the story of a visit to your nearest town. Write about the buildings you saw and the things you did. Perhaps you did some shopping and then went to the public baths or to the amphitheatre. Draw some pictures about your story.

This room has been built in the Corinium Museum at Cirencester. (Corinium was the name of the Roman town at Cirencester.) It shows the kitchen of a house in those days.

Find:

—the raised hearth in the corner

—the iron grid on top of the hearth. Small dishes of food were cooked on the grid over burning charcoal.

—the clay bottle with a spike on the bottom. Wine and oil were bought in these.

—the ladle hanging from the shelf

—the long pot-hanger chain on the wall. Large pots and cauldrons were hung on these over a wood fire.

—the table where the food was prepared.

Roasting and baking were done in ovens. Wood or charcoal was first burned inside the oven to heat it. The ashes were then raked out, and bread, pastries or meat were put inside to cook.

A bronze saucepan

This bowl was used for grinding and mixing food.

The two pictures on this page show some of the fruit and vegetables eaten in Roman Britain. Make a list of those you recognise.

Make a wall picture to show the different plates, jugs, bowls, bottles and kitchen utensils in these two pictures.

The kitchen was a very busy place when guests were invited to dinner.

Favourite Roman dishes were fattened snails and dormice, baked and boiled meats, pigeons, chickens, pheasants, geese and peacocks. Mussels, cockles, oysters and cheese dishes were also popular.

The food was covered with strong sauces, made from spices and herbs. A favourite was a fish sauce made from anchovies. Some of the herbs used were mint, thyme, bayleaf and parsley. Honey was used for sweetening foods.

But the ordinary poor people did not eat so well. Their main food was coarse bread, thick soup like porridge, made from peas and beans, with a little meat when they could afford it.

The knife in this picture is a real Roman knife.

Most of the town houses are now buried under the roads and buildings of our modern towns. But we can still visit and examine what is left of some fine houses that were built in the countryside.

These country houses are called villas. They were often built near the towns, which were their market centres.

Some villas were farmhouses, like the one shown in the picture above. This was near St. Albans. They often had a row of rooms with a corridor along the front or back and sometimes wings of rooms at the end.

Others were fine country houses built around a large courtyard, with sometimes as many as 20 or 30 rooms. You can see one that was built at Chedworth, in Gloucestershire, in *Roman Britain* in the *Focus on History* series.

These houses had their own private bath-houses, with cold rooms, warm rooms and hot rooms, where people sweated to get rid of dirt in their skin. After cooling down, they took a plunge in a small cold water pool.

These large villas were usually the centre of a large farming estate. Near the house were farm buildings for the ploughs, carts and horses, barns or granaries for the corn and vegetables, and huts for the farmworkers. The owner of the estate lived in the villa with his family, or it was the home of his farm manager. The farm work was done by his farm labourers and slaves.

The cattle and sheep provided meat, milk, cheese, wool and leather. Slaves made bread from the corn and wine from the grapes.

Both the large town houses and villas had their own Roman central heating systems. These were called hypocausts. This kind of central heating was used to warm the floors and walls of rooms in private and public bath-houses, too.

Slaves kept the fire burning in the furnace, or stokehole, at the side of the house.

The draught took the heat from the fire between the piles of tiles under the floor of the room. Then the warm air passed up behind the wall-plaster in hollow box-tiles, or flues, to escape through holes in the eaves of the house.

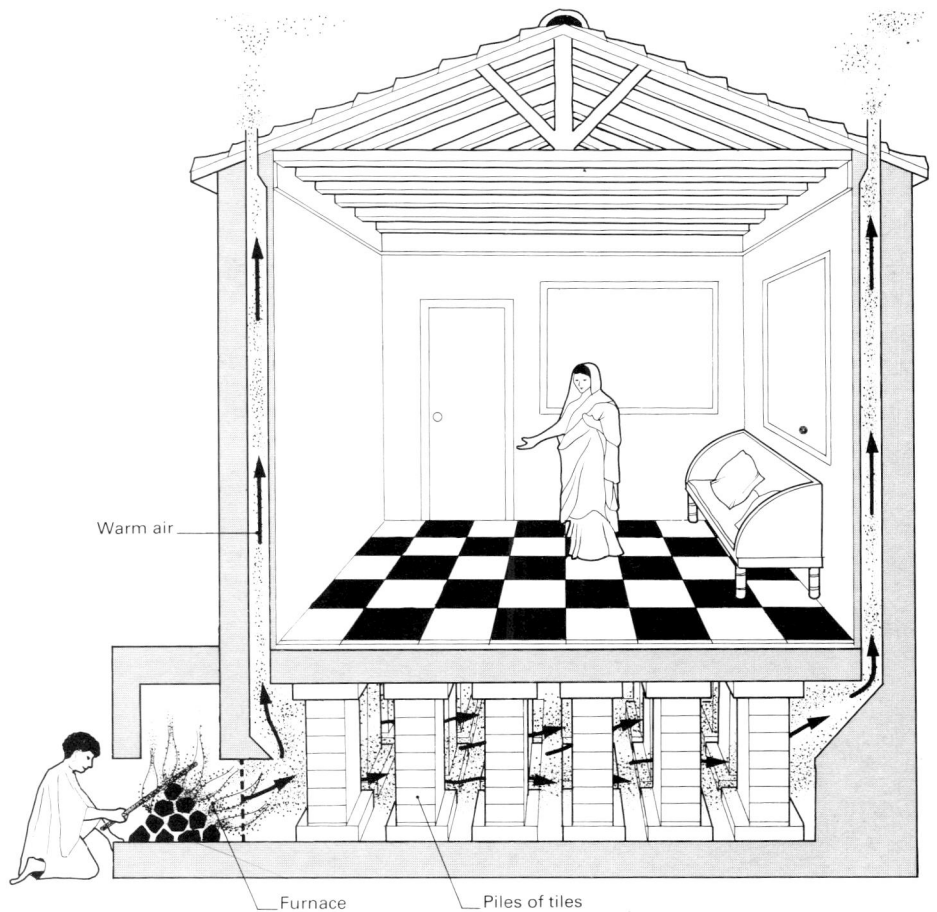

Warm air

Furnace

Piles of tiles

below: The remains of the hypocaust in the Roman villa at Chedworth

Things to do

1 Make a model of a kitchen like the one shown on page 52. Remember to show the hearth, the iron grid, the bottles, the ladles and the table.

2 Make a list of some of the food that was eaten in Roman Britain.

3 Make a model of the hypocaust, or central heating system.

4 Look again at the map of Roman Britain on page 39. Find the name of the nearest Roman town to where you live. Look in other books in your school and local libraries and find out as much as you can about it.

The villas and the larger town houses had reception rooms where visitors were welcomed, dining rooms and bedrooms.

Here is another room built in the museum at Cirencester. This could be used as a reception room or as a dining room.

Find:

—the beautiful mosaic floor, made with small pieces of stone. People chose the pattern they wanted from a book of patterns and then the mosaic floor makers made it for them.

—the painted walls. The ceiling was also painted in coloured patterns.

—the low wooden table, the wicker-basket chair and the wooden couch with cushions. The Romans did not have much furniture in their houses. Couches were also used as beds.

—the figure of a god in the niche in the wall

—the glass window. British craftsmen learned how to make window glass. But fine glass goods, like those on the opposite page, were brought from Gaul and Germany.

Breakfast was a light meal of fruit, cheese and bread. Lunch was usually eaten standing up and it was a cold meal of meat, fish, eggs and vegetables.

The main meal was taken at the end of the day. Then the family and their guests lay on low couches round three sides of a table. Food was served on dishes or platters of wood, pewter, bronze or pottery, and eaten with fingers and spoons.

Wine mixed with water was drunk from small cups. Bread was made at home, or bought from bakeries.

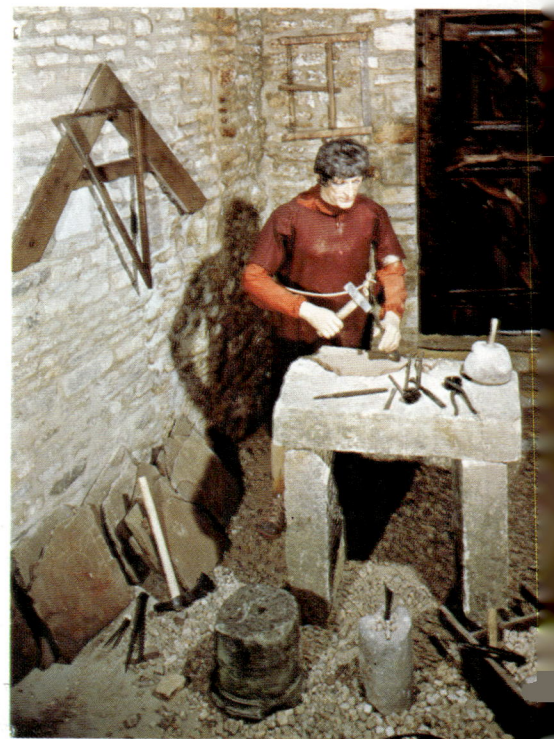

The workshop of a mosaic floor maker

left: A great
silver dish

A clay lamp. It was filled with olive oil
and had a wick of flax or hemp.

below:
Pewter plates

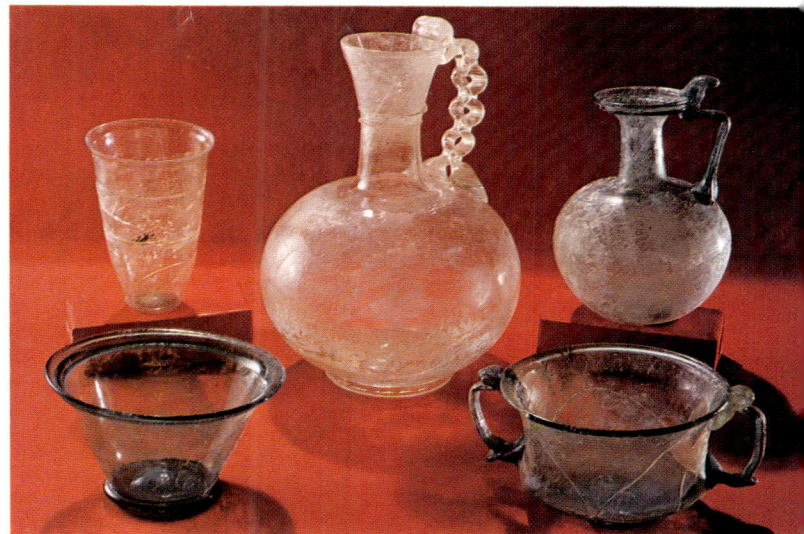

below: Glass bottles
and cups

Feeding-bottles for young children

A Roman
glass bowl

Some models to make

Use these pictures to make your own models. The picture above shows a small farm in the north of England. The ordinary people lived in huts with thatched roofs. The land was still farmed in the same way as in the Iron Age.

Corn had to be paid as a tax to the Romans. This was used to feed the army in Britain and in other parts of the Roman Empire.

Use the pictures on page 56 to make your own models of:
—a Roman dining room
—the workshop of a mosaic floor maker.

A ploughman with his plough and oxen

Religion

The Romans encouraged the Britons to worship Roman gods, such as Hercules, Minerva and Venus.

But many Britons still kept their Celtic gods. The picture on the right shows three Celtic Mother Goddesses. Two are holding trays of food and the other a tray of loaves.

left: Minerva

Soldiers and merchants from the East worshipped a god called Mithras. Temples of Mithras have been found in London and near Hadrian's Wall.

At the far end of the temple was a stone picture of Mithras killing a bull for sacrifice.

The picture on the left is part of a mosaic floor from a villa at Hinton St. Mary, in Dorset. It is now in the British Museum in London. It shows the head of a man who may be Jesus Christ. The sign behind his head shows the first two letters of his name in Greek.

In A.D. 313 the Roman Emperor Constantine made the life and teaching of Jesus Christ the official Roman religion.

This picture was painted on the wall of a room in Lullingstone Villa, in Kent. We think this room was used by the owner as a Christian chapel. It shows people with their arms outstretched in prayer.

Transport

The Roman legionaries built about 9,000 kilometres of roads in Britain. Some of our modern roads are built over them. The Roman roads linked together the forts and towns. Along them, legions marched to where they were needed. Government officers carried messages and collected taxes. Traders moved from town to town. Farmers took their goods to market.

Goods from other parts of Britain and from other countries were also brought in ships to the nearest ports. Then they were sent in river boats, or by road on wagons and packhorses, to the town markets and shops.

Here is a picture of a busy street in Roman Britain.

Look for:
—the donkey with panniers
—the men carrying a lady in a litter
—the oxen drawing a two-wheeled cart
—the horse drawing a covered cart.
What else can you find in the picture?

Here is a model from the museum at Colchester. It shows a
Roman merchant ship at the quayside of the docks.
Look at the picture and find:
—the ship's mainsail
—the sloping poop deck and the goose neck
—the steering oar. There was one on each side of the ship.
—the road leading to the dock
—the sentry on duty at the entrance
—the warehouses on the quayside
—the sacks of corn stacked on the quayside, guarded
   by soldiers.

Parts of a sunken Roman barge have been
found beneath the River Thames at Blackfriars.
This picture shows how an artist thinks it was
used.
Notice:
—the men pulling the barge closer to the
   quayside so it can be unloaded
—the men in a rowing boat pulling the nose of
   the barge.
What else can you see in the picture?

The Romans leave Britain

From time to time Roman Britain was attacked by Picts from Scotland and by Scoti from Ireland.

From about A.D. 270 bands of Saxon pirates sailed across the North Sea to attack ships and raid towns and villas. New forts, now called Saxon Shore Forts, were built along the south and east coasts.

These difficult times were made worse when the Roman armies were moved from Britain to fight in Europe.

By A.D. 410 all the Roman soldiers had left Britain. When the British leaders sent to Rome for help, they were told that they must defend themselves. The Roman-built towns and villas, and the Roman ways, continued for a time, but Britain was no longer protected by Rome and changes were on the way.

Collect together all your notes, pieces of writing, models, charts, pictures and friezes, and make an exhibition of your work, with the title Roman Britain.

Visit museums and places which were once part of Roman Britain. Make drawings and write notes about what you see there. Continue to look in your library for books on Roman Britain, the people who lived there and the way they lived.
Make yourself an expert on Roman Britain.

Part of the walls of the Saxon Shore Fort at Pevensey, Sussex. The castle inside was built later by the Normans.

Index